MARGRET CAREY

BEADS AND BEADWORK OF EAST AND SOUTH AFRICA

SHIRE ETHNOGRAPHY

Cover photograph
Disc necklet 450 millimetres (17¾ inches) wide, strung on wire and worn by married women of the Maasai, Kenya. (Museum of Mankind, London.)

British Library Cataloguing in Publication Data available.

Published by
SHIRE PUBLICATIONS LTD
Cromwell House, Church Street, Princes Risborough, Aylesbury, Bucks HP17 9AJ, UK

Series Editor: Bryan Cranstone

ISBN 0 85263 797 7

First published 1986

Set in 11 point Times and printed in Great Britain by C. I. Thomas & Sons (Haverfordwest) Ltd, Press Buildings, Merlins Bridge, Haverfordwest, Dyfed.

Contents

Acknowledgements

I am grateful to Dr John Mack for reading the typescript and for his advice, and to Bernard Brandham and Dr Jean Brown for help with photographs: also to the following museums and their staff for permission to publish many of the illustrations: Museum of Mankind, London; Pitt Rivers Museum, Oxford; University Museum of Archaeology and Anthropology, Cambridge; Commonwealth Institute, London; Royal Museums of Scotland, Edinburgh; Brighton Museum and Art Gallery; Alexander McGregor Memorial Museum, Kimberley, South Africa. Above all, I am grateful to my husband, for his support.

The cover picture and plates 2, 3, 6, 14, 15, 23, 25, 26, 27, 28, 29, 31, 32, 35, 36, 37, 42 and 43 were photographed by Michael Bass. Plates 11, 18, 19, 21, 22, 33 and 40 (top left) are by the author. The map on page 6 is by D. R. Darton.

List of illustrations

1
Introduction

The beads chiefly used in African beadwork are glass, mostly made in Venice, Italy, and Jablonec (Gablonz), Czechoslovakia. Trade in these beads started in the seventeenth century and has profoundly influenced the costume of eastern and southern Africa. Hitherto, personal ornament had relied on natural materials such as feathers, skins, plaited fibres and seeds as well as body painting and scarification. Records and pictures show that before the nineteenth century the Zulu peoples wore virtually no beads but made good use of ostrich feathers and decorative skins. In the 1830s traders and visitors presented beads in quantity to the Zulu chief Dingane in exchange for ivory. Some of these beads were bestowed on members of the court, while the bulk were used to adorn Dingane, his wives and his royal kraal or stored in his treasury. While such beadwork is indeed early, it cannot be called truly traditional since it arises out of an introduced material.

'Traditional clothing' as described in the following pages is therefore a relatively recent development and on the whole refers to clothing and ornament unmodified by accompanying European-style wear.

While beading is a woman's craft almost everywhere in the area covered by this book, beads themselves, when not imported, are usually made by men, though both sexes wear beadwork.

The area defined as east Africa for the purpose of this survey comprises the Sudan and the Horn of Africa, Rwanda, Uganda, Kenya and Tanzania. Southern Africa includes Zambia, Zimbabwe, Malawi, Botswana, Lesotho, Namibia and the Republic of South Africa, with a note on Madagascar.

This book gives some historical background, places beadwork within its tribal context and gives some criteria for provenancing.

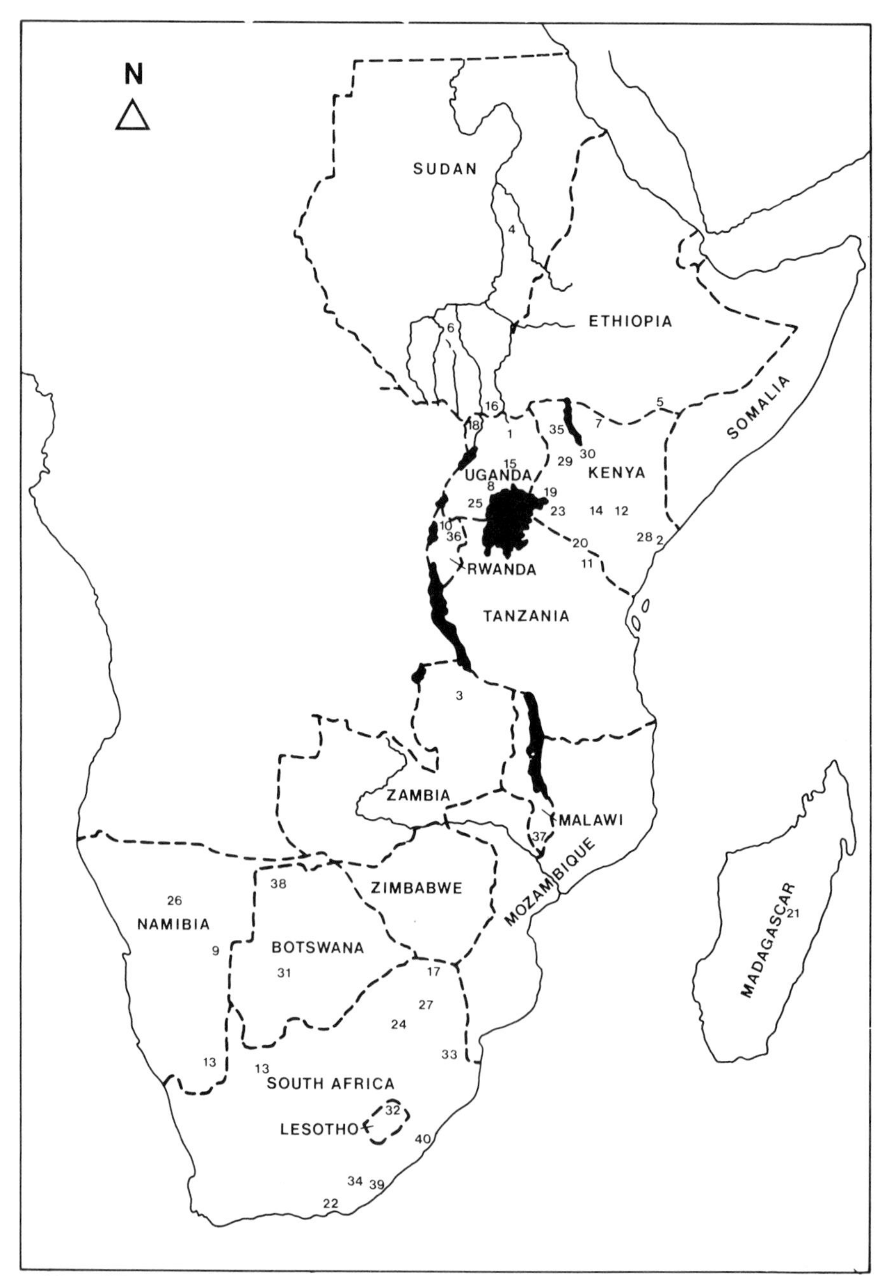

Map of East and South Africa showing countries and tribes mentioned in the text. Tribes shown are: 1 Acoli; 2 Bajun; 3 Bemba; 4 Bisharin; 5 Borana; 6 Dinka; 7 Gabbra; 8 Ganda; 9 Herero; 10 Hima; 11 Iraqw; 12 Kamba; 13 Khoikhoi; 14 Kikuyu; 15 Lango; 16 Lotuxo; 17 Lovedu and Venda; 18 Lugbara; 19 Luo; 20 Maasai; 21 Merina; 22 Mfengu; 23 Nandi; 24 Ndebele; 25 Nyoro; 26 Ovahimba and Ovambo; 27 Pedi; 28 Pokomo; 29 Pokot; 30 Samburu; 31 San; 32 Sotho; 33 Swazi; 34 Tembu; 35 Turkana; 36 Tutsi; 37 Yao; 38 Yei; 39 Xhosa; 40 Zulu.

2
Beads

The English word 'bead' comes from the Old English *biddan* (to pray) and refers to the beads on a rosary. The *Oxford English Dictionary* defines 'bead' as 'a small perforated body, spherical or otherwise, of glass, amber, metal, wood, etc, used as an ornament, either strung in a series to form a necklace, bracelet, etc, or sewn upon various fabrics'.

Almost all beads have to be made, whether from organic materials like ivory, animal teeth, bone, shell, wood and seeds, from mineral sources such as stone, clay and metal, or, most importantly, from glass.

Seeds were already the right shape and needed simply to have a hole bored; making a bead from stone, metal or shell might take a long time. Where iron was not available, an awl made from a pointed stone, bone or thorn was set in the hollow end of a reed and rotated between the palms, often using an added abrasive of moistened sand. Such a drill has a conical point; drilling was done from both sides and the hole has an hourglass-shaped cross-section; often the two parts are not quite in line. This technology was adequate for short perforations. Longer (10 millimetres, 3/8 inch, or more) holes came after the arrival of iron in east and southern Africa and the use of iron awls. Ironworking reached the Zambezi valley in about the first century AD. Iron awls must have revolutionised bead making since they were hard, could be sharpened easily and could be used to make longer, narrower holes. Heated, they could char through wood and seeds.

Therefore, before glass beads were imported in quantity, beads were relatively uncommon, highly valued, and usually took a long time to make. Certain types of bead, and the earliest trade beads, were the preserve of chiefs, though beads themselves are less important than skins, teeth and claws of lions and leopards as a mark of rank. In southern Africa lion and leopard teeth were made into beads; such a necklet could only be worn by a chief or warrior, likewise with leopard claws, which Africans copied in brass and bone (fig. 1); porcelain imitation teeth were made in Jablonec.

Many sorts of shells were used in bead making, of which ostrich eggshell is the commonest, found almost everywhere in the area. Beads are made by chipping a shell fragment to the approximate shape and drilling a hole. After some blanks had been pierced,

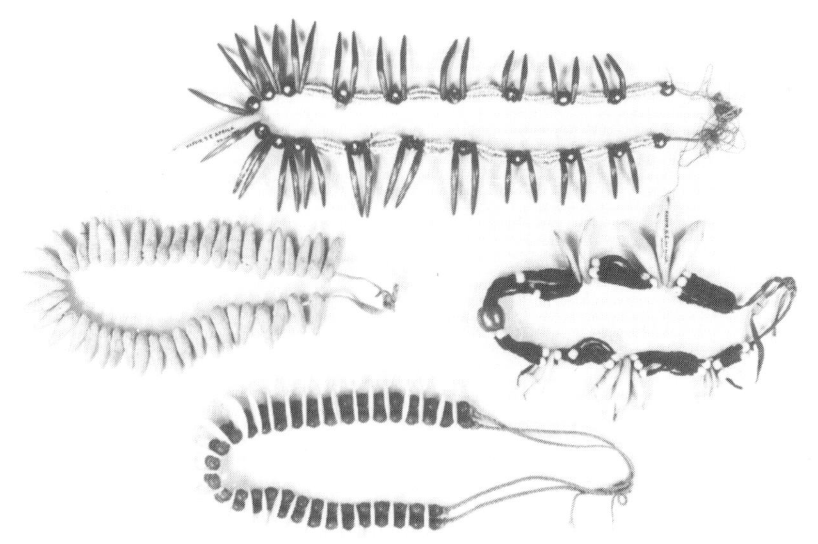

1. *(above)* Necklets with feline claws and teeth, South Africa, probably Xhosa. (Top) Brass imitation claws. (Centre, left) Clay beads imitating teeth. (Centre, right) Real teeth. (Bottom) Bone imitation claws. (Copyright: Pitt Rivers Museum, University of Oxford.)

2. *(below)* Series to show the stages in making ostrich eggshell beads as made in Mwanza district, Tanzania. (Museum of Mankind, London.)

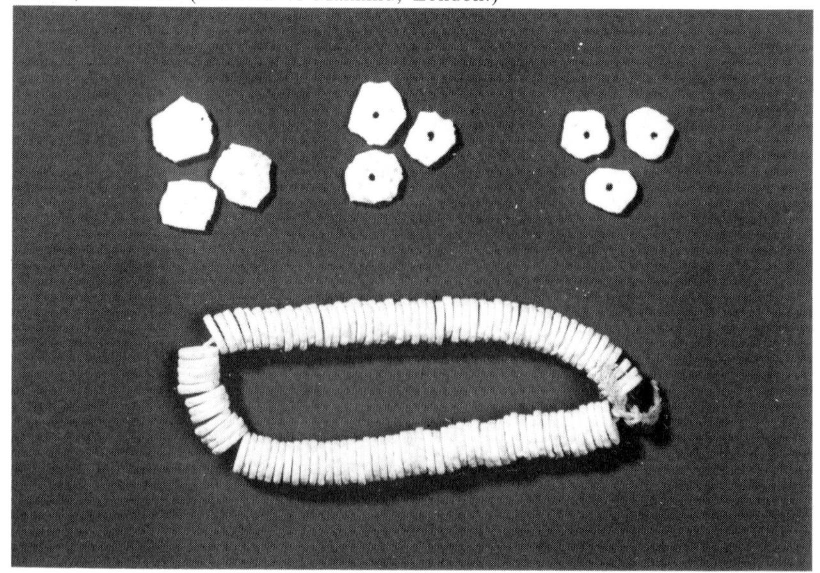

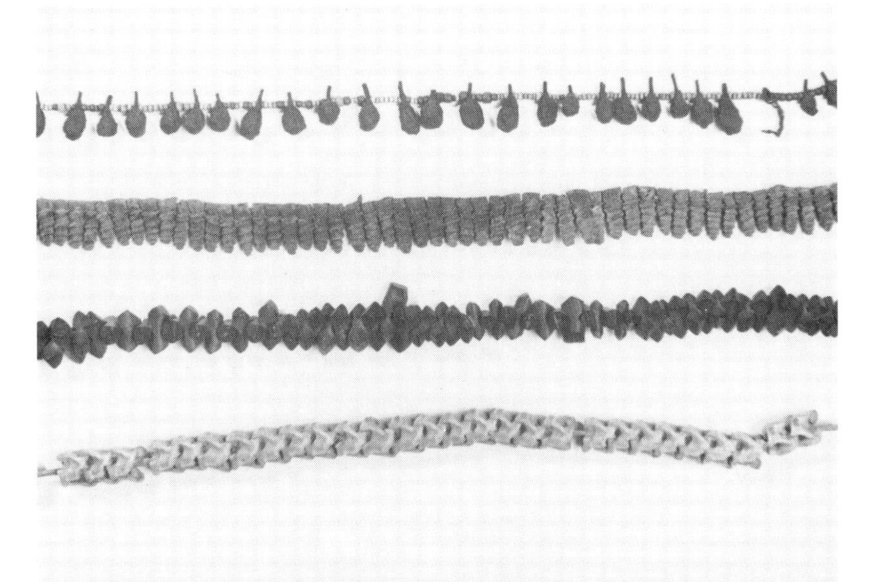

3. Natural materials used as beads: small tubers (Kikuyu, Kenya); rolled-up fragrant leaves (Kikuyu, Kenya); bobbin-shaped wooden beads, an award for killing an enemy (Zulu, South Africa); and snake vertebrae (Maasai, Kenya). (Museum of Mankind, London.)

they were strung on a cord and rubbed along a grindstone till they were a satisfactory finish and size (fig. 2). In the Sudan the discs were soaked in water to prevent splitting during their perforation with an iron awl. A man could make one hundred beads in a day. Such beads were sold by the string (about 60 inches or 1500 millimetres), which might hold over one thousand beads and double that number if made of the thinner shells of the giant African land snail or fresh-water clam or mussel. Ostrich eggshell beads are white and flat; snail and clamshell beads are greyish, thinner and slightly concave. Coconut shells make similar discoid beads.

The Kikuyu of Kenya make perfumed beads from rolled-up leaves, small tubers or roots (fig. 3); the fragrant wood of the tambootie tree *(Spirostachys africana)* is used in southern Africa to make rod-shaped beads. The Sotho make small sun-dried beads of clay mixed with vegetable perfume.

In southern Africa long ropes of bobbin-shaped wooden beads may imitate snake vertebrae and are worn as an award for courage; snake vertebrae are necklets among the Dinka and Luo; plastic 'snake' beads are modern.

Metal is a favourite bead-making material, since it is durable and polishes well. Such beads were nearly all African-made; the metal was also often mined and smelted by Africans.

Glass beads form the largest group of bead-making material found in Africa. Almost without exception, they are imported, yet they have become so thoroughly integrated that they are now a basic part of African costume and ornament.

Glass is a mixture of silica (typically sand) and an alkali fused together. Chemical and spectroscopic analyses are important in archaeological studies since visually identical beads may be chemically distinct and widely separated in date and provenance, especially with favourite types.

There are three basic methods of making glass beads. *Wound* beads, where the glass, while still plastic, is wound round a wire mandrel, are perhaps the earliest. They can be recognised by the swirl marks and tiny air bubbles encircling the hole. *Drawn* beads are made by trapping an air bubble in a lump of molten glass, which is then pulled out to make a long slender tube. Beads are made by chopping such a tube into the required lengths, and several tubes can be cut at once. Round beads (also called 'seed' or 'pound' beads) all belong to this group, though the grain, which runs parallel to the hole, is not noticeable except in striped beads. They are the commonest single type in Africa. Early beads have sharp edges, showing that they have not been tumbled in a heated drum; they are also more irregular in length and angle of cut. *Moulded* beads are a later development and include plastics, a twentieth-century innovation. They can be recognised by the 'seam' of the mould.

The earliest glass beads are thought to have been imported from India by Arab traders, perhaps since 200 BC. These beads, found on east African beaches and archaeological sites, have been named 'trade-wind beads'. They are made of opaque glass coloured black, brick red, dull yellow, green or greenish blue and are either wound or drawn. The Portuguese called them *barros miudas* (earthenware beads). As the Dutch built up their colonial empire in the east, the importing of trade-wind beads declined, and from about 1680 beads came from Europe, especially from Venice and Amsterdam. Beads were imported by the shipload during the eighteenth and nineteenth centuries, when they were a principal currency. Even in the 1950s the Zulu imported some 40 tons of beads annually.

By the fifteenth century Venice had a well established glass industry, with monopoly laws to keep the craft within Italy.

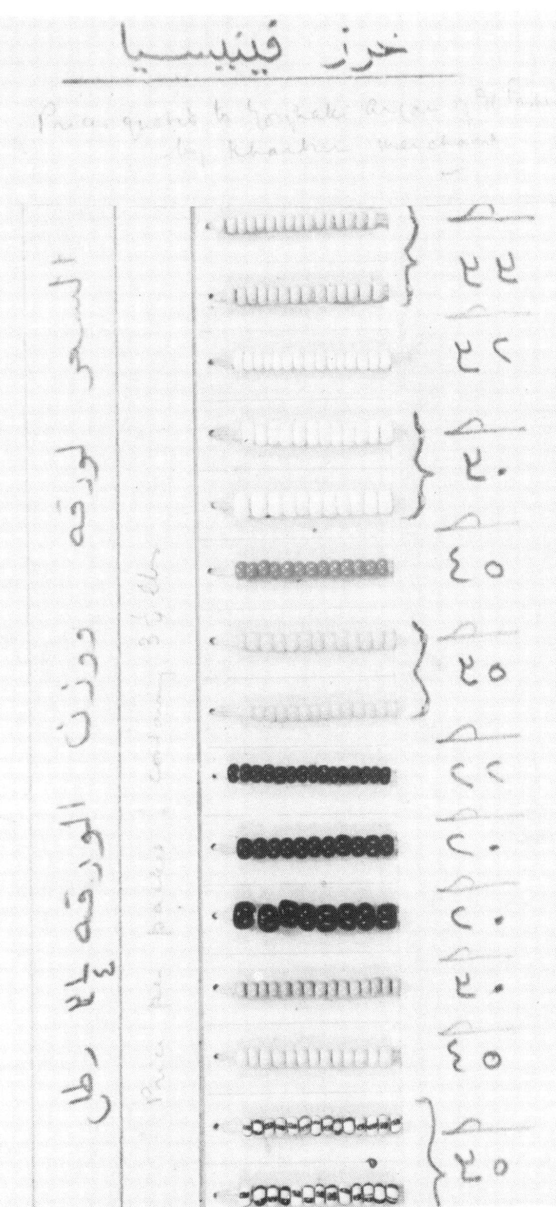

4. Sample card of Venetian beads annotated in Arabic with the prices per 3¼ pound (1.47 kg) packet by a Khartoum merchant selling to a small tradesman in the Sudan. (Copyright: Pitt Rivers Museum, University of Oxford.)

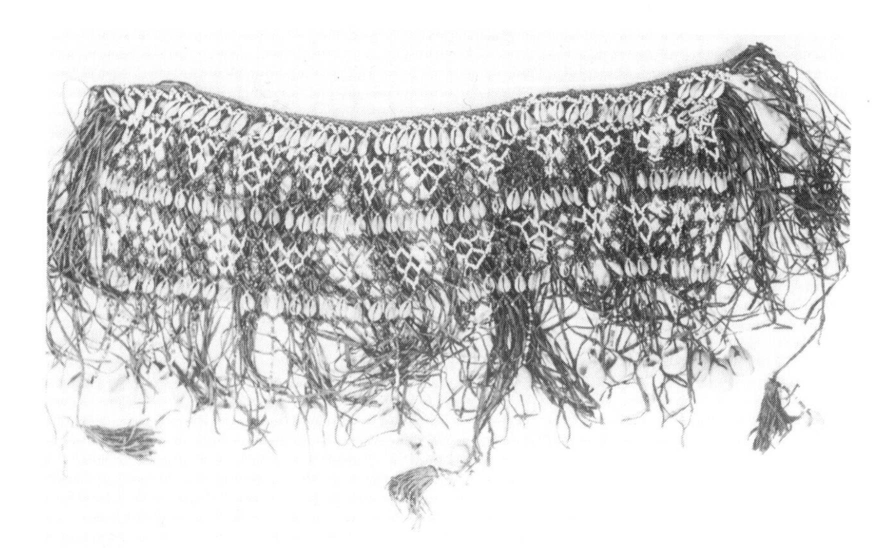

5. 'Nubian' fringed apron, *rahat,* probably from the Bisharin of the Sudan. (Copyright: Pitt Rivers Museum, University of Oxford.)

Nevertheless an Italian set up a glass house in London in 1549, and in 1640 an Englishman got a patent for 'the sole making and venting of Beads and Beaugles'. In Amsterdam a glass industry flourished in the seventeenth century, and by the sixteenth century bead furnaces appeared in Bohemia.

London and Antwerp were both ports to which beads were imported for re-export elsewhere, as customs records indicate. Arab and Indian traders bought European beads which came by the shipload to Zanzibar. H. M. Stanley, the explorer, writing in 1872, calculated that for a two-year period he would need twenty-two sacks of beads, and that eleven varieties ought to cater for local differences in taste between Zanzibar and Lake Tanganyika. Beads were measured in *khete* (a necklace length) and one *khete* bought a day's rations for a porter. Ten *khete* made a *fundo,* used for large purchases. Beads were threaded on palm-leaf fibre strings and were carried in long narrow sacks weighing two *frasilah,* equalling 70 pounds (32 kg), or one porter's load. One 70 pound bag of red *sami-sami* beads (the most valuable) cost 26 dollars in 1871.

Although an estimated four hundred different varieties of trade beads were manufactured in the mid nineteenth century, each tribal group might accept no more than five to ten colours, sizes or shapes. The commonest, the round or 'seed' bead, might be available in seventeen sizes from 1.5 millimetres to 10 millimetres in diameter ($\frac{1}{16}$ to $\frac{3}{8}$ inch) but in practice only four or five sizes are found in east and southern Africa.

Beads were selected from catalogues which were often sample cards with actual beads. The Museum of Mankind, London, has a leather-bound sample book and annotated bead sample cards of the mid nineteenth century. Sample cards are numerous; the Tropical Institute in Amsterdam has a few hundred such cards, incorporating several thousand different beads, which represent the range once available through a merchant firm trading in Amsterdam, and which came from Venice and Jablonec. Such cards enabled Europe-based merchants to make their choice; even an Arab trader in the Sudan might own one (fig 4).

6. 'Kissar' type beaded lyre 1.04 metres (3 feet 5 inches) high, with leather-covered wooden bowl, from the Sudan. (Museum of Mankind, London.)

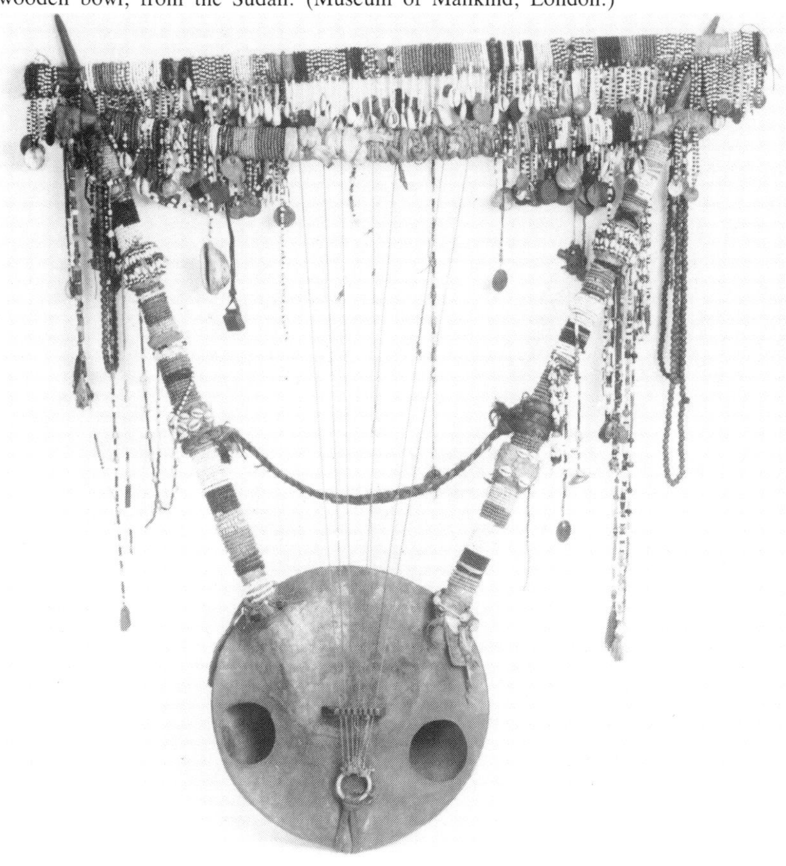

The methods and materials used in stringing beads can give an indication of date. In general, a twisted thread of vegetable fibre or sinew or a thin leather strip is a sign of traditional method, and a piece of beadwork with such threading is unlikely to be more recent than 1945. Machine-made thread, usually cotton, indicates a twentieth-century date, perhaps after 1925 at earliest, but along the east African coast the use of cotton in beadwork does not necessarily mean a recent date since there is a long-established tradition of using cotton, which is due to contact with Arab culture. The use of a beading needle and wire-strung beads is fairly recent.

Beads may be strung singly or built up into a flat fabric by linking one bead at a time to an existing row or series of rows. Such a fabric slightly resembles a brick wall in that lines of beads are parallel in one direction and stepped or herringbone-wise in the other. Openwork bead fabric may come as strands linked by bar spacers, strung in a netted trellis pattern (figs. 5, 35) or with an ornamental picot edging (fig. 26). Flat beadwork strips that may have been made on some sort of frame are found along the east African coast from Kenya down to Malawi, in the Arab culture contact area (figs. 19, 21). These may be distinguished by the way the beads lie parallel along the length and width of the strip, the presence of a bead selvedge, and the cotton warp threads forming knotted ties at each end. They appear to have the beads on a single weft thread held in place by a double-thread warp and could have been made on a simple loom or by finger weaving.

In applied beadwork the beads may be sewn on individually, as prepared medallions attached to a base, or by 'lazy stitch', where up to twelve beads at a time are threaded and secured by a small stitch through the base material (figs. 17, 25, 32). It is a good way of beading a large surface rapidly. Beads can also be applied as a continuous thread wound round and round the object to be covered (fig. 40), or as a separate meshed or close-stitched cover (figs. 15, 37).

3 East and central Africa

The interior of eastern Africa was somewhat isolated from outside influences until the first half of the nineteenth century. This may partly explain why the beadwork of east Africa has a different character from that of southern Africa, and why beads made of locally available materials such as seeds, iron and ostrich eggshell are used proportionately more.

The first imported beads came from the east by means of Arabs who traded along the coast, especially between the Red Sea, Lamu and Dar es Salaam. Agate and carnelian beads from Cambay in western India have been imported for almost two thousand years and were common in the Sudan. Later, Indian glass beads, which may have come from the ancient Chola kingdom west of Madras, were imported between about AD 850 and 1518. Beads, cloths and brass from India were probably traded for ivory, gold, slaves and rhinoceros horns.

European glass beads seem to have arrived in this part of Africa later than in southern Africa and in smaller quantity. To begin with, trade contacts were with Arab and Indian merchants in the coastal areas. Travellers stocking up with supplies before setting out for the interior would buy large quantities of beads from Indian or Arab merchants, especially at Zanzibar. Ujiji, on the east shore of Lake Tanganyika, where Livingstone was found in 1871, was an Arab trading base.

THE HORN OF AFRICA

The Horn of Africa has two zones of beadwork: the Ethiopian interior, and the coastal areas comprising Eritrea and Somalia. There is not much beadwork, perhaps because the people wear woven clothing, but many women and children wear a necklet of trade beads. In Ethiopia silver was used to make jewellery and numerous small bell-shaped pendants for the rims of ceremonial baskets. Rich Somali women might wear silver bracelets and necklaces; silver charmcases to hold a Koranic text could be worn by both sexes. The necklace in fig. 8 is composed of a silver charmcase with filigree ornament and pendant drops, together with Venetian glass beads and chunks of copal. This would be a dowry necklace and might be passed from mother to daughter. Copal is the semi-fossil resin of an extinct tree, dug up on the Zanzibar coast. Imitation copal beads have been made in

Jablonec from butter-yellow glass; more recent plastic or resin imitations come as long cylinders that can be cut and polished as required. Such cylinders have been bought in Nairobi as 'Somali amber'. Jewellery of this sort belongs to the Islamic culture area and is made by professional silversmiths. The silver, which is impure, is worked into hollow spherical or biconical beads, chased, plain, or covered with filigree. The old girdle from the Bajun of Lamu (fig. 18) on the Kenya coast is made of black, yellow and white trade beads, coral beads and silver spacer bars. The coral is said to have come from Arabia and is rare in east Africa, while the vertical spacers form a link with the beadwork found in the hinterland.

THE SUDAN

The Sudan forms a bridge between the Islamic culture area and inland east Africa. The northern part of the country is inhabited by Moslems; a beadwork style called 'Nubian' probably comes

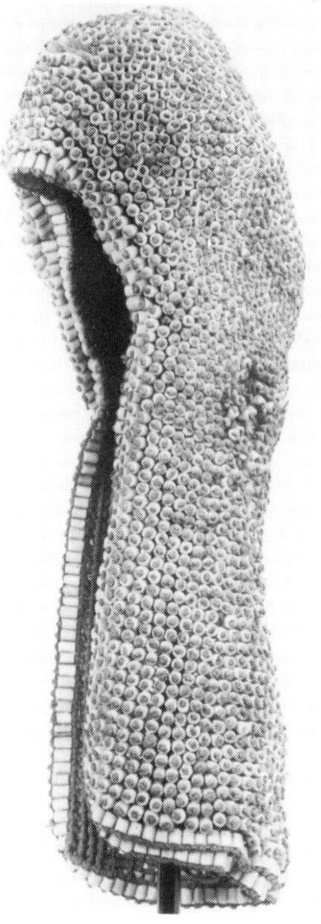

7. Man's headdress ascribed to the Nuer of the Nilotic Sudan. The style, a skullcap with integral neck covering, is most unusual for the area and may perhaps reflect external inspiration. (Copyright: Pitt Rivers Museum, University of Oxford.)

8. Dowry necklace with copal beads, glass trade beads, silver beads and charmcase. Somali-Arab work of pre-1900 date. (Copyright: British Museum, London.)

from the Bisharin peoples. Examples of this are waist aprons (fig. 5), usually in a net-like mesh of white, brick red, yellow and green beads with rows of cowrie shells on a leather fringe backing. The lyre in fig. 6 is similar to Ethiopian ones used during ceremonies to cure the sick by driving out the devils. The beading is 'Nubian' with a row of cowries hanging from the top; it is also hung with a Koranic charm, Moslem rosaries and coins, mostly piastres of the 1880s, with one British 1861 penny. Such a lyre would have been used at weddings and other rituals.

South of Khartoum, the Nilotic Sudan and its peoples mark a transition. Traditionally, men and unmarried girls (for example, Dinka) wear minimal clothing, which might include a string of beads round waist or neck. Necklets of old Venetian beads are a sign of wealth. Because of the greater abundance of trade beads in recent times, some Dinka men wear bead 'corsets', in which the torso is tightly cased in multiple strings joining in a dorsal

9. Royal drum decorated with cowries, red, white and blue trade beads and a separate 'crown' with colobus monkey fur tufts, from the Ganda of Uganda. (Copyright: Cambridge University Museum of Archaeology and Anthropology.)

10. *(left)* Royal crown beaded in red, white and blue beads, with a false beard made of colobus monkey fur, from the Nyoro of Uganda. (Copyright: Pitt Rivers Museum, University of Oxford.)
11. *(right)* Woman's skin apron from the Turkana of Kenya, with large glass beads and an iron bead border. (Cambridge University Museum of Archaeology and Anthropology.)

spine. These corsets indicate their position in the age-set grading. Marriageable girls may wear loose cape-like bodices similarly made of bead strings, covering shoulders and body down to the navel, with a central contrast band vertically down the centre. Red, pink, purple, yellow, turquoise blue and black beads are used according to age-grade and sex.

Where few clothes are worn, body decoration, including elaborate men's coiffures, is important. Samuel Baker describes (1867) how the Lotuxo (Latuka) of the southernmost Sudan 'wear most exquisite helmets' made on a foundation of the owner's hair. 'The framework . . .completed, it must be perfected by beads, should the owner of the head be sufficiently rich . . . The beads most in fashion are the red and the blue porcelain, about the size of small peas. These are sewn on to the surface of the felt, and so beautifully arranged in sections of blue and red that the entire helmet appears to be formed of beads . . .' Such

12. A Turkana woman at Lokitaung wearing bead head, neck and breast ornaments and a skin apron similar to that in fig. 11. (Copyright: Richard Beatty.)

headdresses might be worn only by warriors who had killed in battle; later they were a mark of seniority and made detachable. In northern Uganda, the Lango peoples wear skullcaps of felted hair decorated with ostrich eggshell beads and small black seeds, later on with white trade beads; the Acoli have spherical caps of felted hair with applied beadwork on small leather discs. The headdress in fig. 7 is made of off-white tubular glass beads attached to a string foundation twined into an open rectangular mesh. It was collected between 1850 and 1865 by John Petherick and is ascribed to the Nuer, who live north-east of the Dinka in the southern Sudan. The clay-based headdresses worn by men of the Turkana of northern Kenya and the neighbouring Karamojong of north-eastern Uganda are complemented by beaded browbands, chinstraps and ear ornaments.

EAST AFRICAN BEADWORK

Over most of this part of east Africa, men's clothing is a skin cloak worn with a belt, necklet, browband and armlets, some of which may be beaded; the men tend to dress more plainly with seniority. Chiefs may own clothing appropriate to their status. The Luo chief in fig. 13 is photographed wearing a beaded skin cloak and 'heirloom' beads which set him apart from his people and may form part of his regalia. Some men's dance costume was beaded, such as the iron beanpod-shaped rattle worn on the outer thigh at young men's dances among the Kikuyu. Beads form only a small part of the spectacular head, neck and breast ornaments worn by men of the western Kenyan Luo at dances and ceremonies, which are made up of numerous hippopotamus and warthog tusks.

While details vary between groups, a woman's traditional clothing indicates her position within the cycle of marriage and childbearing. An unmarried girl usually wears a hip skirt, sometimes beaded, and a skin cloak; from puberty onwards she might begin acquiring beaded neck and head ornaments. After marriage, she tends to cover her breasts, whether with an accumulation of necklets, a beaded leather strip or a skin cloak. A leather pubic apron, triangular or rectangular, is often ornamented with cowries and other beads in proportion to the husband's wealth; this may be worn hidden beneath the leather back skirt which has the two ends overlapping on the woman's stomach. Some of these skirts are beaded with trade beads or locally made iron beads and are worn on ceremonial occasions or at weddings. The most striking of these come from the Iraqw of

13. A senior chief of the Luo, north-western Kenya, wearing a beaded leather cloak and 'heirloom' beads. (Copyright: Pitt Rivers Museum, University of Oxford.)

Tanzania (fig. 17); white, red, blue, yellow and black beads applied in lazy stitch make an extremely heavy and prestigious garment.

With married women, bead ornaments concentrate around the neck and head. Neck rings, whether of palm-leaf fibre, threaded seeds, metal, glass or plastic beads, may totally cover the neck and shoulders. The Samburu of Kenya reckon that a woman does not have enough necklets unless they support her chin. The amount of ornament and beadwork on head and neck is a measure of a woman's status and her husband's means. Since women often shave their heads, their large, variously shaped ear ornaments, headbands and necklets have maximum visual impact.

Cowrie shells from the Indian Ocean are used from the Sudan and the Horn down to Tanzania and valued as a costly import or as a symbol of fertility and increase, since the shell's slit is likened to a woman's sexual organs. They are used as pendant or appliqué beads, on female clothing, especially pubic aprons, on royal insignia and in other contexts where prosperity is important.

Iron beads made by bending a short band into a ring with a butted join are common in eastern Uganda and northern Kenya and are used in multiple necklets, women's 'tails' and garment edgings, either by themselves or with cowries, ostrich eggshell or glass beads. Trade beads with large perforations are often used

14. (Left) Rattle worn on the thigh by young men at dances. (Right) A *rira* apron worn in pairs (one in front, one behind) by initiated women. They are usually kept hung up as an ornament. Kikuyu of Kenya. (Museum of Mankind, London.)

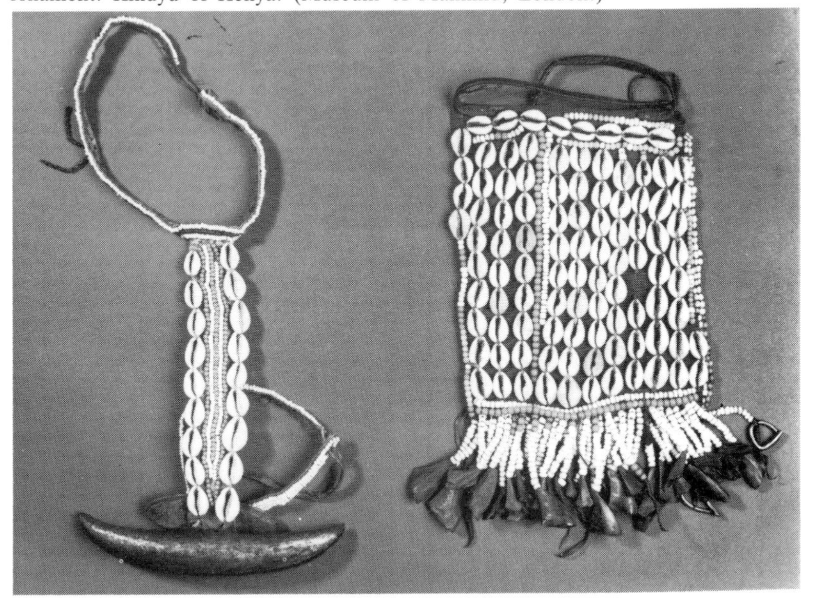

since beading is generally with leather strips. The commonest are white, turquoise, blue or red round beads; blue, green or yellow ring beads; or blue faceted so-called 'Russian' beads. The Gabbra and Borana of northern Kenya wear strings of faceted beads made of aluminium, but formerly of soft stone, which may be a local copy of 'Russian' beads.

Culture traits are often shared by more than one tribal group; broadly similar beadwork links the peoples of north-eastern Uganda and northern Kenya, while the Samburu, Maasai, Nandi and Kikuyu over the southern half of Kenya and the northern half of Tanzania in their turn have many similar pieces of beadwork, often using lengths of iron chain. The Maasai are perhaps the only ones whose women wear large discoid necklets threaded on wire (fig. 16); these succeeded flat quoit-shaped necklets and, before that, single-strand necklaces.

Kamba beadwork is a bridge between that of the interior and that of the coastal areas, since flat beadwork is found among both. Beadwork strips, often finger-woven on long warp threads, are made as girdles from the Pokomo of Kenya down to the Yao

15. Bead-covered gourds from the Maasai (left) and the Kamba (right) of Kenya. The Kamba gourd, part of a bride's dowry, is used when she feeds her husband for the first time. (Museum of Mankind, London.)

16. Maasai married woman wearing beaded ornaments including a disc necklet similar to that shown on the front cover of this book. (Copyright: Jean Brown.)

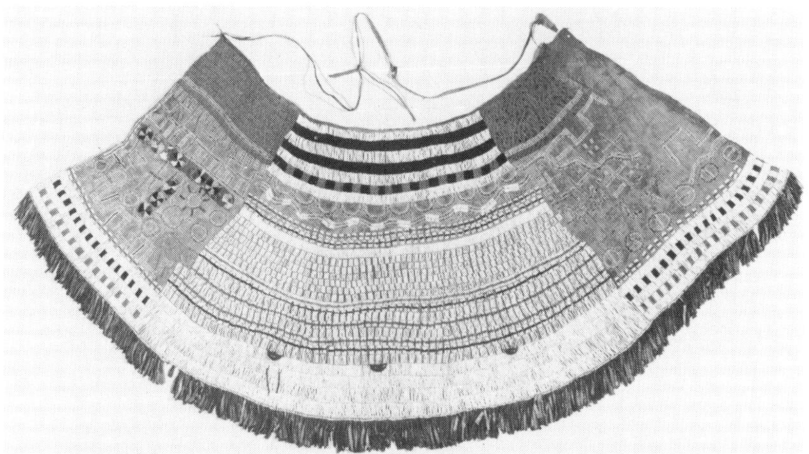

17. *(above)* Woman's wedding skirt from the Iraqw, northern Tanzania, made of four skins heavily beaded in bands and symbolic designs. (Commonwealth Institute, London; copyright British Museum.)
18. *(below)* Old girdle of coral and glass beads with silver spacer bars from the Bajun, near Lamu, Kenya coast. (Cambridge University Museum of Archaeology and Anthropology.)

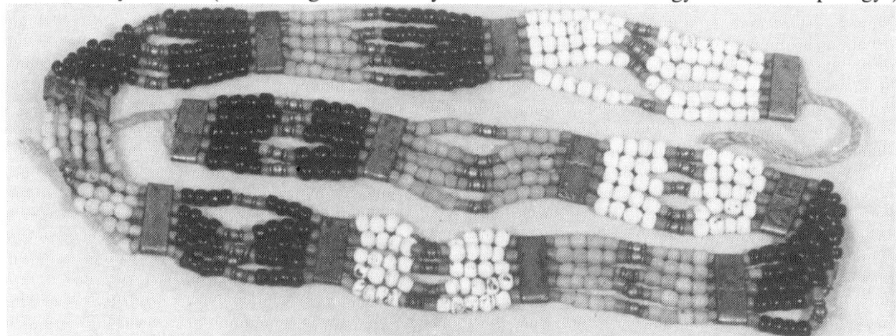

of Malawi (figs. 19, 21). Colours give a clue to provenance since the Pokomo favour red, white and dark blue; in Tanzania pink, light and dark blue, white and black are used, while the Yao fancy lilac. Combs decorated with beads and bead panel aprons are found in the coastal and Eastern Bantu areas. The girls in fig. 20, apparently from somewhere near Dar es Salaam, are wearing distinctive fringed bead aprons, and gauntlets made of beads, buttons and cowries.

Vertical spacers are a feature of east African beading; the Pokot use small bones or aluminium lengths in girdles; the Maasai and Nandi use hide spacers in beading gourds.

The colours of older east African beads were limited to white, black, navy, royal and pale blue, red and scarlet; now yellow, orange and green in several shades and also clear beads are added to the colour range. Oval, discoid and 'snake' beads are recent. Aluminium beads and pendants are twentieth-century introductions, probably after 1920, and commoner still after 1945.

Beads made from the flattish base of *Conus* shell varieties from the Indian Ocean were highly valued throughout east and central Africa and were often reserved for royal or ritual use. They are either circular, using the whole base, or triangular, made by cutting the base in half and grinding it down. Ivory and bone imitations made in central Africa (fig. 22) are doubly exclusive, since ivory is usually a chief's perquisite. European porcelain imitations are common.

THE INTERLACUSTRINE BANTU

A distinctive style of beadwork is found among the Interlacustrine Bantu, a group living to the west and north of Lake

19. Beadwork from the Pokomo of Kenya: headband (top), neck ornament (centre) and girdle. The design on the necklet includes fecundity symbols. (Cambridge University Museum of Archaeology and Anthropology.)

20. A 1920s photograph of girls from eastern Tanzania. (Copyright: Pitt Rivers Museum, University of Oxford.)

21. *(above)* Pubic apron (upper left), girdle (lower left) and beaded combs (right) from the Yao of Malawi, showing affinity with the beadwork found in the east African coastal area. (Cambridge University Museum of Archaeology and Anthropology.)
22. *(below)* Royal necklet (pre-1900) made with glass trade beads and triangular ivory beads made to imitate the rare *Conus* shell from the Indian Ocean. Bemba of Zambia. (Royal Museums of Scotland, Edinburgh.)

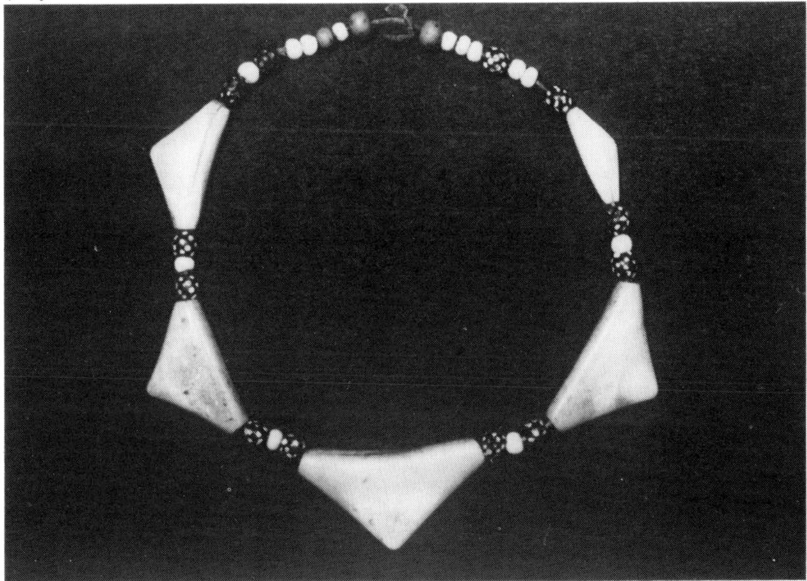

23. Nineteenth-century imitation crocodile-tooth amulets and beaded arm rings showing the tiny beads characteristic of old Malagasy beadwork; and a protective charm taken from a dead soldier. (Museum of Mankind, London.)

Victoria, in Uganda and Rwanda. They include the Tutsi (Watussi), Nyoro and Ganda. The Hima royal dancers have been filmed and photographed, rhythmically tossing white manes of colobus monkey fur in their war dance. They wear headbands, chinstraps, collars and bandoliers beaded in basketry-derived patterns of triangles, lozenges, chevrons and bands in white, black and blue beads.

Dance headdresses and costumes may be worn by whoever can afford them; the *Ekondo* beaded crown headdresses are worn only by titular chiefs and certain nobles. Such crowns (fig. 10) are made of coiled basketry covered on the outside with beads in traditional designs, usually in red, white and blue, or in white with blue or black. Some have a crest or false beard of colobus fur. A Tutsi crown has a string face veil ending in blue and white beaded pendants.

Royal ladies and noblewomen made fine basketry in their leisure hours and also covered royal emblems and insignia with beadwork in white, blue, red and black. Drums (fig. 9), harps, trumpets, flutes, spears, headbands, face veils and hair ornaments could also be beaded in the same style.

4
Southern Africa and Madagascar

MADAGASCAR

Madagascar, one of the world's largest islands, is often included in books dealing with African culture as a matter of geographical convenience. Its population and way of life are a mixture of Indonesian and African elements, with many local variations.

Excavations at a village destroyed just after 1500 showed that the inhabitants had imported large numbers of carnelian and glass 'trade-wind' beads from India. Subsequently, in the seventeenth century, Dutch traders imported beads from Amsterdam.

There is no beadwork in Madagascar to compare with that found in east and southern Africa. Perhaps this is because Madagascar has a strong textile tradition; the wearing of beadwork seems to have more affinity with cultures where skin clothing was customary. The Merina in central Madagascar wore bead necklaces and also *haba,* the rare armlets made from cotton or hemp rings covered with tiny beads (about 1 millimetre, 1⁄32 inch) in black, red, yellow, orange, green, blue and white, patterned in lozenges and isosceles triangles (fig. 23). The armlets appear in a portrait of the 1820s.

Beads tended to be used on charms or in association with them, usually in the form of bands on to which the tiny beads were sewn (fig. 23). The best known are the crocodile-tooth charms (whether made with real or imitation teeth) worn by members of the ruling or military class. In Madagascar the crocodile is the largest, strongest and most dangerous animal; its teeth could give the wearer strength in the same way as lion or leopard teeth, claws and skins do in Africa. Other charms with bead sleeving are cattle horns, small horns containing 'medicine' or small carved figures; these might be used to avert danger, bring good luck or work spells. In recent times Arab traders in the principal towns sold European beads from Venice or Jablonec as charms for a variety of purposes.

ZIMBABWE: ANCESTRAL BEADS

Some excavations in stone-walled ruin sites in Zimbabwe were carried out in the belief that the ruins were over two thousand years old and belonged to Ophir, the source of King Solomon's gold. Radiocarbon dates from subsequent more scientific excava-

tions provide a chronological framework for the finds, which include gold beads, imported Indian beads and trade beads from Europe. The bead-producing layers are dated approximately 1050 to 1700. Gold beads are very small, under 3 millimetres (1/8 inch) in diameter and are of local manufacture. Most of the beads seem to have come from India and may have come from factory sites in the ancient Chola kingdom west of Madras. Dates for these factories are about AD 850 to 1518. Some of the beads, which fall into the 'trade-wind' bead group, might be the original 'beads of the water', the ancestral beads revered among the Venda.

The Venda, an offshoot of the former inhabitants of the Zimbabwe ruins area, moved to their present home in the Transvaal in about 1700. Venda 'heirloom' beads are believed to represent the ancestors; in the event of any trouble the witch-doctor or diviner finds out which ancestor is angry and points out the relevant bead. Its owner then has to carry out appeasement rituals, which include blowing on the bead with water to 'cool' it. Venetian trade beads, some no older than the mid nineteenth century, are among the 'heirloom' beads. Witch-doctors make others of brass, copper and iron strips bent into rings. Butted ends indicate a male ancestor, overlapping ends a female.

24. *(opposite)* Photographed in 1923, this Southern Ndebele bride wears a beaded *linaga* cape, a *nyoga* strip and other bead ornaments. (Copyright: Duggan-Cronin Collection, McGregor Museum, Kimberley, South Africa.)
25. *(below)* (Left) Bride's apron, *jocolo*. (Right) married woman's apron, *mapoto*. Stylistically the *mapoto* is the older piece. (Museum of Mankind, London.)

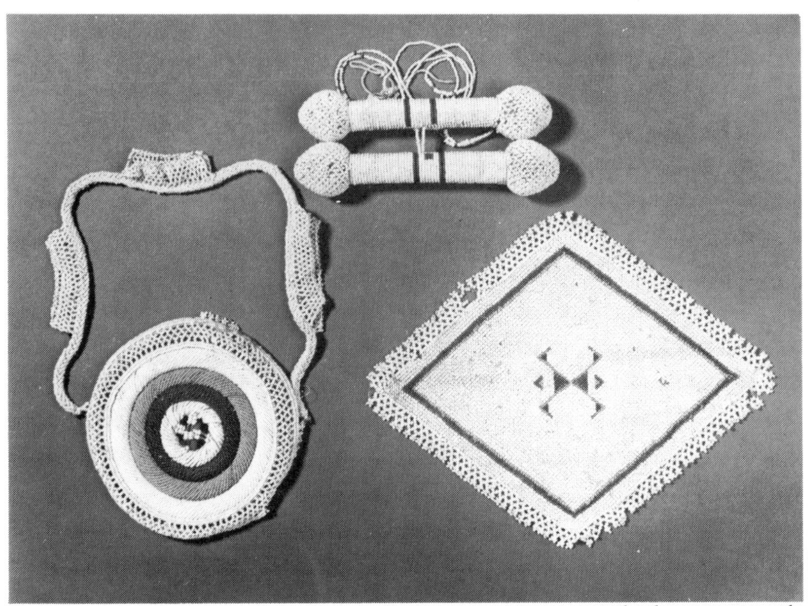

26. Ndebele bridal beadwork. (Left to right) Breast ornament, upper back ornament and a head covering as worn by the bride in fig. 24. (Museum of Mankind, London.)

The best known Venda ancestral beads are the *vhulungu ha madi* — 'beads of the water' (or sea), which may refer to a foreign provenance. They are translucent rather than transparent and are mostly pale blue, blue-green or blue-grey; the translucency is almost as if a waxy cloud was trapped inside the bead. A string of these is threaded so that the irregularly cut ends meet and the result is more like a flexible glass cord than a string of beads. Early 'beads of the water' might have come from one of the Indian factories, but a European provenance is more likely since trace elements of cobalt and antimony date them to the sixteenth century and later. Suggestions of Phoenician origin are not now thought likely.

An heirloom bead, ivory amulet or cowrie shell might form the centrepiece of a necklace made of many bead strands, half yellow on one side, half blue on the other, which is worn by women who have undergone the Venda *domba* school initiation.

Heirloom beads also occur among the Lovedu and Pedi of the Transvaal. The Lovedu Rain-Queen used in her rain-making rituals beads which may antedate 1800, the traditional date of the southward migration from Zimbabwe. Pedi heirloom beads are reserved for royalty and nobility. They are small drawn beads which may have come from Italy via Portuguese traders in Angola; similar ones are found among the Ovambo and Herero of Namibia.

TRANSVAAL NDEBELE

The Transvaal Ndebele have an individual style of beadwork. They are not the same as the Zimbabwean Ndebele (better known as Matabele) and they are divided into two groups, northern and southern. The northern Transvaal Ndebele can almost be classified as Sotho; the southern Transvaal Ndebele have two subtribes, Manala and Ndzundza, and are locally called Mapogga after a former chief. They are based near Pretoria.

The southern Transvaal Ndebele are probably best known for the geometric paintings on the walls of their houses and courtyards. Originally the women executed these in earth colours (white, black, blue-grey, yellow and red ochre) and the paintings had to be renewed annually. Now they tend to use shop-bought oil paints in white, red, green, yellow, blue and black, giving a wider and more vivid palette. These paints are more weather-resistant and need renewal only every three years. The formerly geometric designs came to include stylised house facades with

27. (Above) Headband made of ostrich eggshell beads from the San. (Below) A girdle of ostrich eggshell and red glass beads from Lesotho, probably San work, acquired in 1870. (Museum of Mankind, London.)

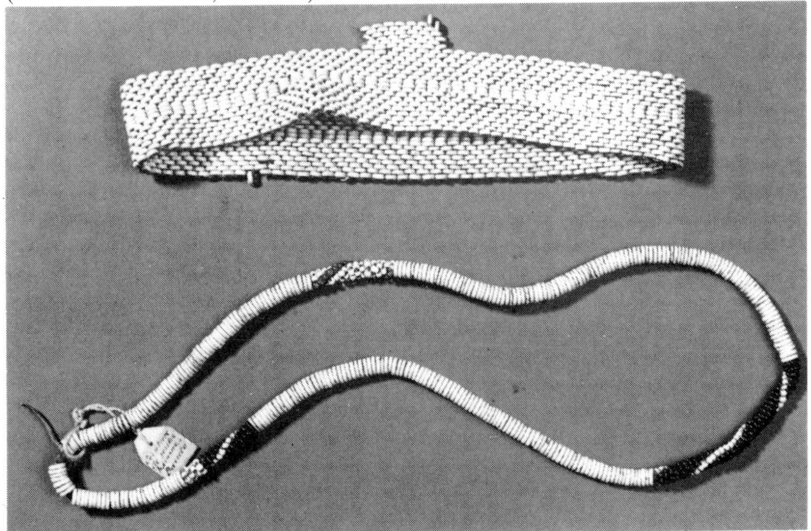

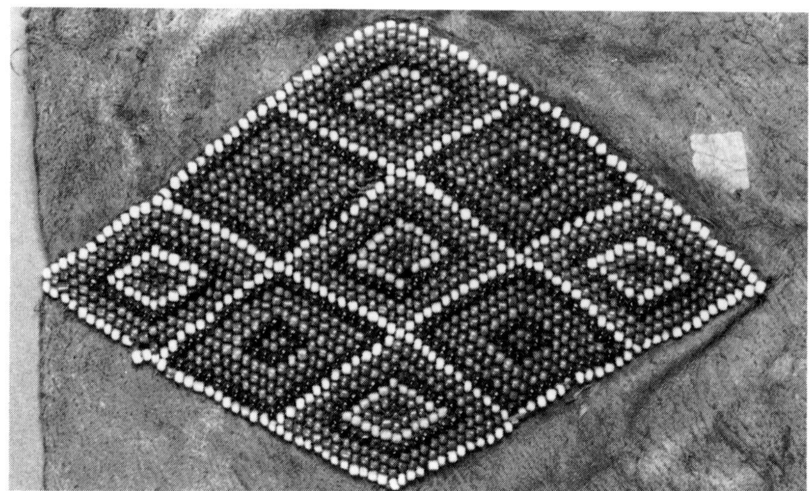

28. Medallion of beads sewn in lozenge design on to a skin garment of pre-1910 date from the Khoikhoi, South Africa. (Museum of Mankind, London.)

furniture and lettering; the whole effect has become much more exuberant.

A similar trend appears in Ndebele beadwork. The oldest may go back to the late nineteenth century. Traditionally the capes, aprons and skirts were made of sheepskins decorated with small white beads and including a few red and blue ones, sewn on with sinew threads in lazy stitch. The holes in these small beads are too small to allow the use of a needle; sinew thread is stiff enough to pass through directly and the only tool needed was an awl to pierce the skins. Beadwork in this style may have continued until about the 1940s. As more beads became available, the ratio of beaded to unbeaded skin increased, and in perhaps the late 1940s and 1950s beads began coming in a larger variety of colours to include red, pink, orange, yellow, green, blue (light and dark), black and white, many of them transparent. The beads also came in a larger size, allowing the use of needles and machine-made thread. Beading became less time-consuming and was used more extensively. Designs became bolder and included, for example, house outlines and car number plates; they also took up more of the beadwork area, though still against a white background. In about 1970-1 colour preference shifted towards opaque beads, mostly green, blue, purple, brown and black, with few white beads, thus creating a rich and sombre effect. The material used in making women's aprons also changed, the traditional skins being replaced by leather backed with canvas or even canvas alone, whether in single or double thickness. A later development is to make the same aprons in the same designs, but in different-coloured plastics cut out and glued together, with braid and trimming added. Such an apron can be made in a few hours; the earlier traditional garments must have taken weeks or even months to make.

As so often in African societies, beadwork is worn mostly by women and as a girl progresses towards her married, adult status, so her clothes and ornaments change. A small girl wears a *ghabi,* a beaded panel about 240 millimetres (9½ inches) wide with a geometric motif, above a fringed apron of cord or leather threads which is attached to a beaded loin band. She might also wear a full pleated skirt with bead trimmings called a 'scotch' and, for dress occasions, a small beaded bodice. As she grows older she may get larger-sized replacements and at puberty she will have a *pepetu,* a rectangular apron averaging 380 millimetres (15 inches) wide by 280 millimetres (11 inches). Older ones on a skin backing are quite flexible; canvas *pepetu* are as stiff as boards. The girl's mother makes it, and she wears it on her coming-out day together with other bead ornaments that she has made herself, such as buttock coverings, a long triangular back skirt, a short bodice, and beaded hoops for neck, body, arms and legs.

At marriage there is a fresh array of beaded clothing and ornament. The *pepetu* is replaced by the *jocolo* (fig. 25), a rectangular apron about 440 millimetres (17¼ inches) across by 600 millimetres (23½ inches) long, the lower edge ending in five finger-shaped panels. A *jocolo* is the first symbol of married status and is later worn on special occasions. A bride's finery will also include a *linaga,* a sheepskin cape, sometimes with the fleece left on the inside, more or less heavily beaded in white according to its date and the desire to make an impressive effect. Two *nyoga* (meaning 'snake'), long flexible strips made of white beads with a few small geometric motifs in colour and between 1 and 1.5 metres (3 feet 3 inches to 4 feet 10 inches) long, are attached to the bride's shoulders on top of the cape, or, as shown in the 1920s photograph (fig. 24), one in front and one behind. A bead headdress or headband and numerous neck, arm and leg ornaments might be added; she will also carry small baskets and a beer gourd decked with white beads, a beaded wedding stick and a fertility doll. Until all ceremonies have been completed, the bride must remain covered under a blanket, which may have a broad edging of white beads (symbolising purity) applied with the picot border that is so characteristic of Ndebele beadwork.

After the first few months of married life a woman is entitled to wear the *mapoto,* a rectangular beaded apron (fig. 25) about the same width as the *jocolo* and 450 to 550 millimetres (17¾ by 21¾ inches) long. It has a rectangular tongue at each corner and a leather fringe filling the space between.

The upper part of *pepetu, jocolo* and *mapoto* aprons is folded forward so that a supporting belt can go through the seam thus made. The older aprons are mounted on a flexible waistband following the body shape; later fashion and stiffer foundations cause aprons to be worn like a flat panel standing away from the body on either side.

In addition to the bead clothing already described, Ndebele women make beaded hoops to wear on neck, body, arms and legs, sometimes covering most of the person. These hoops are made of grass, the whole surface being covered with a continuous string of beads wound in the closely packed diagonal spiral that characterises Transvaal beaded hoops. Such hoops are sometimes built on to the body and are removed only at a husband's death. Similar hoops on fertility dolls, wedding sticks and dancing sticks make them instantly recognisable as Ndebele. In the 1930s hoops were narrow, 20 to 40 millimetres (¾ to 1½ inches) thick depending on diameter; now a woman's beaded neckring may be 120 millimetres (4¾ inches) deep, with silver or brass studs added, looking rather like a surgical neck support. Bead pendant panels and other ornaments worn on breast, back or forehead, headbands, necklaces and chestbands are all part of the optional wardrobe. Necklaces are sometimes made of carved oblong panels of fragrant tambootie wood; these or picot-edged bead panels are strung on a lace-like band of white beads. On special occasions a married woman may wear a cloak made of a store-bought blanket totally encrusted on the outside with beads and weighing up to 10 pounds (4.5 kg). The beads alone would have cost about 7-8 rand in March 1983 so that such a blanket involves a considerable outlay in cash as well as time and trouble.

In contrast to the finery worn by women, who pose for tourist photographs, Ndebele men wear European-style clothes for every day. On special occasions, such as entering 'boy's school' (a form of initiation) or attending a wedding, they may revert to a more traditional style of clothing — a loinskin and multiple ropes of red, white and blue beads worn like bandoliers crossed over shoulders and chest, and beaded headbands.

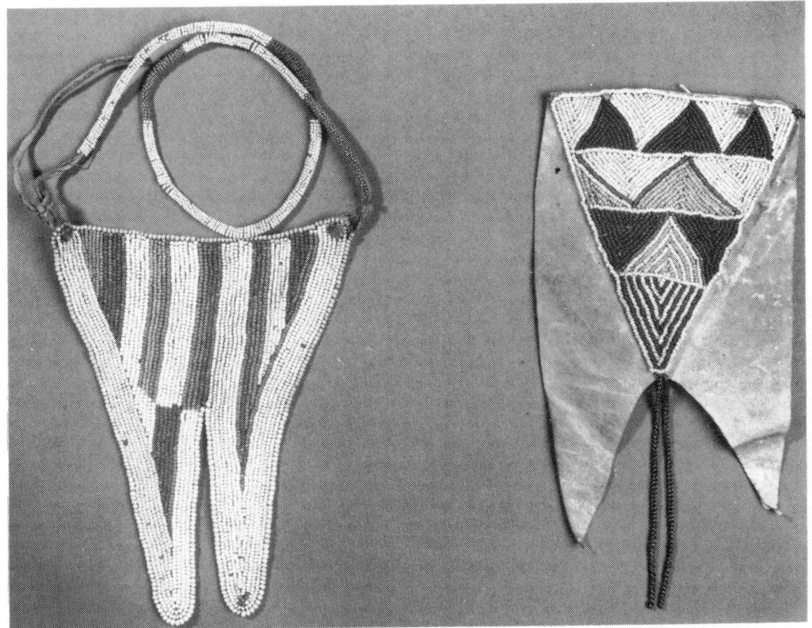

29. Women's aprons, probably from Lesotho, beaded in 'lazy stitch'. The one on the left dates from the 1850s; the other is a later style. (Museum of Mankind, London.)

SOUTHERN AFRICA'S EARLIEST INHABITANTS

Southern African beadwork is rich in diversity of pattern, ornament and colour but it is difficult to survey coherently. This is partly due to tribal movements, which were scantily documented before the later nineteenth century, and partly because beadwork artefacts were attractive and portable mementoes. Proper provenancing was minimal.

With the help of early studies by German missionaries at Mariannhill in Zululand, old photographs, typological analysis and the more detailed researches of present-day students, it is possible to work out a framework for the tribal attribution of beadwork. This is far from complete, and, especially among the Cape and Natal tribes, there is considerable intermingling of styles, artefacts and colour preferences to cloud the issue.

The San are the oldest surviving people of southern Africa. Formerly they occupied practically the whole area but they are now reduced to small groups living in the Kalahari desert of Botswana and Namibia or in native reserves. They are hunter-gatherers: the men hunt while women collect vegetables, seeds, fruits, larvae and small animals for food. The San and their way of life have been under pressure over the past millennium by Khoikhoi and Bantu invaders from the north. When the Dutch East India Company, during the seventeenth and eighteenth centuries, founded a settlement at the Cape for use as a provisioning station for the East Indies trade, they came into contact with the San, whom they called 'Bushmen' (or wild men), and the Khoikhoi, whom they called 'Hottentots' because of their clicking speech.

The San and the Khoikhoi are quite closely related, with similar physical characteristics and 'click' language, but the Khoikhoi are taller and have a more settled, pastoral lifestyle. They are thought to be the result of a mixture of San and Bantu that occurred much further north, and they too used to live over much of southern Africa. Dutch settlers traded with Cape Khoikhoi for cattle and sheep in return for metal, cloth and beads. The San had no trade contact with the Dutch; instead, they were hunted down and killed, especially whenever they shot or stole cattle grazing on their tribal hunting grounds.

San beads are made by the women out of ostrich eggshell; they are smaller and more finely finished than those made anywhere else in Africa, being only 5 to 7 millimetres (3⁄16 to 1⁄4 inch) in diameter. Such beads are used on the edges of soft, dove-grey skin garments, as tassels on tortoiseshells containing *buchu* (a vegetable perfume) or in headbands (fig. 27) and single-strand girdles. Ostrich eggshells were precious water containers in the desert and would only be used to make beads if they got broken. The need to make the best possible use of the shells perhaps accounts for the smallness of San beads.

Although the San had no trade contact with Europeans, they did get a few glass beads via the Khoikhoi, so some San ornaments such as tortoiseshell containers may have a fringe of glass beads with tiny triangular pendants (fig. 37).

The Khoikhoi, who were exposed to European contacts from the seventeenth century, have left few identifiable examples of their material culture; we have to rely on early travellers' descriptions to know what they wore. Sparrman, writing in the 1770s, describes them wearing headbands with cowrie shells, necklaces of *Nerita* shells (a sea snail) and girdles of ostrich eggshell beads. 'They very much fancy, and ... purchase the glass beads of Europe, especially the blue and white ones the size of a pea', which they wore as a string roung the waist. The Dutch also traded brass beads imported from Java when glass beads became a drug on the market. The Museum of Mankind has a few skin garments called 'Hottentot' (or Khoikhoi) which have beadwork applied in concentric diamonds of white, red, orange, yellow, blue, dark blue and black trade beads (fig. 28). They could have come from a London Missionary Society station in the Ciskei or near Kuruman. Present-day Khoikhoi survive in Namibia and northern South Africa as Nama, Korana and Gonaqua.

LESOTHO AND BOTSWANA

Information on beadwork from Lesotho (Basutoland) and Botswana (Bechuanaland) is patchy, and there is relatively little identified from these areas in museums in Britain. The Sotho are one of the southern African Bantu peoples who may have come from the Transvaal. They make fertility dolls which can be recognised by the use of beads in a soft butter yellow. Some pieces combining large and small round beads in alternate lines may be Sotho; narrow forked aprons beaded in white with black, dark or pale blue on a skin backing, mostly from the nineteenth century, are perhaps Sotho, though it is not known whether they are front aprons or worn on the back as in more recent Sotho costume. Skin cloaks and skirts with circular bead medallions are Sotho style; girl initiates of the *Bale* school wear cane face masks partly beaded over.

In Botswana some beadwork is mixed with small ostrich eggshell beads, thus showing contact with the San (fig. 27); the Yei of north-east Botswana make back skirts in black and white beads which consist of bead strips in geometric patterns hanging from the broad beaded waistband over a leather fringe. The rare older ones had ostrich eggshell beads from the San; the women do the beading while men make the leather skirts.

NAMIBIA

There is not much on record about the beads and beadwork of Namibia, formerly German South-West Africa. The principal tribal groups are the Ovambo and the Herero, living in the northern half of the country, and the Nama, a Khoikhoi group, in the south. The Ovambo and Herero are Bantu cattle herders, whose womenfolk used to wear leather clothes and now wear a version of early twentieth-century dress introduced by German missionaries' wives.

Ovambo women may wear massively heavy 'saddles' of multiple strands of ostrich eggshell beads with vertical hide spacers. Old trade beads are used as an alternative to ostrich

30. Women of the Herero in Namibia, wearing traditional leather clothing and heavy iron and ostrich eggshell beadwork.

eggshell beads in the saddles, on back aprons and necklets, or to ornament a baby's carrying cape or a woman's elaborate coiffure. Such old beads tend to be larger than those generally used in southern and south-eastern Africa, being about 5 millimetres (3⁄16 inch) in diameter. Other old beads are small drawn tubular beads, often dark red, green or black, which may be used in covering fertility dolls.

Like the Ovambo, Herero women's traditional dress included multiple strings of ostrich eggshell beads, made into heavy 'corsets', and similarly made anklets and necklets made with iron beads strung on thongs. Iron beads are made of a short strip about 7 millimetres (¼ inch) wide bent round a solid leather thong and are tooled to give a slightly segmented appearance. A married woman's traditional dress was all of leather, with a remarkable headdress having three 'ears' rising about 250 millimetres (10 inches) above the crown (fig. 30). It is now obsolete, but women of the related Ovahimba, living in Ovamboland, still wear iron bead anklets, necklets and breast ornaments and *Conus*-shell pendants with their leather clothing.

XHOSA BEADWORK

The Xhosa-speaking peoples live along the south-eastern seaboard of southern Africa. They were the first Bantu to meet the Dutch settlers and were generally called 'Kaffirs', a derogatory term from the Arabic *kafir* (unbeliever); their older beadwork is often labelled 'Kaffir' or 'South African Kaffir'.

Xhosa country is divided into Ciskei on the west and Transkei to the east. In Ciskei the Mfengu (Fingo) are the largest group; they were originally refugees *(imfengu),* the remnants of several tribes who fled southwards from the Zulu. Mfengu favour pink beads, so that Xhosa-style beadwork in pink, pale blue and white is likely to be from Ciskei or the Mfengu. Necklets with one or more beadwork rectangles, usually in white with a design in red, pink and blue, with stylised animal or human figures, are likely to be Mfengu; and they use white pearl or china buttons on skirts and blankets.

31. Iron beaded head ornament (left) and ostrich eggshell 'corset' (right) strung on leather thongs, from the Herero of Namibia. (Museum of Mankind, London.)

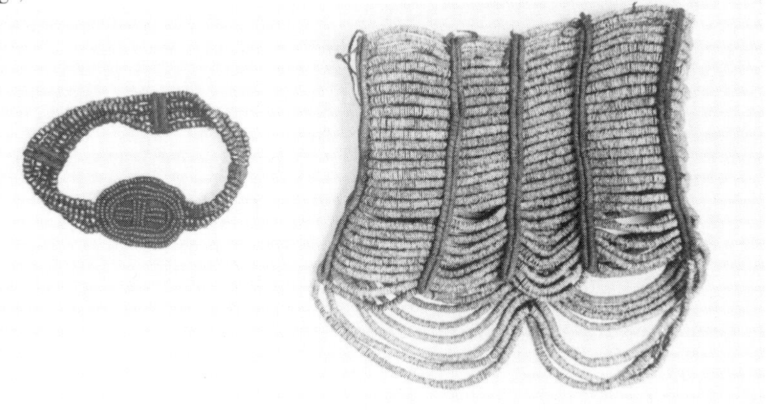

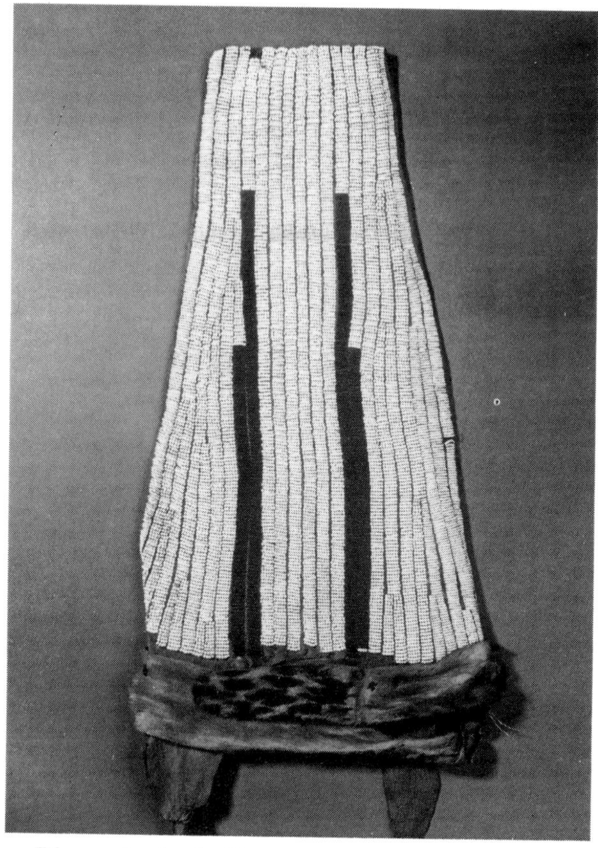

32. Woman's festive bonnet, worn hanging down the back, and secured with skin wrap-round ties, of the mid nineteenth century, from the Gcaleka of South Africa. (Museum of Mankind, London.)

The principal Xhosa-speaking tribes of the Transkei are the Gcaleka (Galika), the Tembu (Tambookie), and the Mpondo (Pondo). The Ngqika (Gaika) live on both sides of the Great Kei river. As the Xhosa-speaking peoples share many similarities, they will be treated as one group.

In museums, a few old skin garments with bead edgings survive, and one item of old Xhosa costume that is not rare has been variously described as a quiver and as a baby-carrying sling. It is, however, a married woman's cap for wearing at gala occasions (fig. 32). The beads, applied in lazy stitch, are normally white with dark contrast, and the style derives from the women's skin caps described by early travellers. Another old-style Xhosa garment is the bead fringe worn by married women as a breast covering (fig. 33). Older Xhosa beadwork is in two colours only,

33. Old-style woman's breast cover of bead strings over a thick cotton backing, from the Xhosa of South Africa. (Cambridge University Museum of Archaeology and Anthropology.)

usually white with black or dark blue; white with pale blue may indicate a later date.

Present-day Xhosa clothing consists of blankets and a heavy cotton baize often described as 'Kaffir sheeting', which is usually white or dyed black. The blankets and much of the cotton baize are coloured with red ochre in shades varying according to the tribal group. Xhosa beadwork is often identifiable by the pink stain of red ochre, which is the 'blood of the earth' and is used in honouring the ancestors. Anointing with red ochre from infancy onward affirms membership of the tribal group.

A small child wears a bead string round its middle which is added to and is a measure of its growth; charm necklets help teething and ward off illnesses. Small girls wear beaded pubic aprons, boys wear bead waistbands.

34. The wives of the king of the Ngqika who was defeated in 1878, wearing bead clothing including breast coverings similar to that in fig. 33.

Puberty marks a great increase in the amount of beadwork worn. Beading is an occupation for women, especially teenage girls, who make ornaments for themselves and their boyfriends. Courtship is often begun by the girl; if she fancies a young man, she will make him three headbands, all to be worn together if he accepts the first one. As the affair progresses, the girl makes arm and leg bands, numerous belts and neck ornaments ranging from chokers to necklets with one or more panels, whether square or elongated. Young men working at the mines bring back black rubber rings or washers that, when beaded, make handsome collars. A 'waistcoat' is made of bead strip panels, linked by strands of white beads to cover the ribs and pass over the shoulders, buttoning down the front. Face masks incorporate 'spectacles' and hoop earrings and are worn by unmarried youths and girls. A purse, safety pins, mirror, snuffbox and whistle are a few of the things that a girl will bead for her beloved. Men continue to wear bead finery after their marriage on special occasions; one man may own over seventy-five pieces of beadwork made to fit and to be put on in proper sequence. Tembu men's bead colours include green and yellow, which stand for new life and fertility.

Girls after initiation and before marriage wear a short skirt and beadwork including headbands with long bead fringes, hoop earrings linked by bead strings looped over face and head, a variety of neckbands, necklets and collars, waist girdles and buttock girdles. A young girl, bride or childless woman may wear a small beaded fertility doll.

After marriage, a woman has considerably less beadwork, wears a longer skirt and a large turban and covers her breasts. Married men and women are entitled to wear wide flared collars and may now smoke pipes with long, not short stems; the stems may be fully beaded instead of having a short beaded collar.

Xhosa *amagqira* (witch-doctors, diviners or herbalists) may be women or men. They are expert in herbal medicine and provide protective charms for all occasions. If men, they wear European clothes with just a string of white beads to denote their calling, but in full dress the costume includes a white skirt (short for a man, long for a woman), white bodice or bead waistcoat and many white beads in a waterfall over the chest, as an eye veil and down the back, a long string wound round the wrist, headbands, anklets, and on the skirt. Charm necklaces, an animal-skin headdress, flywhisk with beaded handle, beaded staff, tobacco pipe, medicine gourds and horns are all part of the insignia.

A man's bag has a straight-lipped opening and three compartments for money, tobacco, pipe and matches, while a woman's bag has V-shaped lips. Such bags are usually white, made of heavy cotton, sometimes of leather, with lines of beading and bead or thong fringes.

Favourite modern Xhosa colours include a great deal of white, pale or turquoise blue, with navy blue, black and bright red contrast. Beadwork worn by unmarried youths and girls may have tufts of cerise wool. Patterns are usually simple: lozenges, chevrons, zigzags, horizontal or diagonal lines against a white background; the overall effect is one of light clear colours.

While the Xhosa do not have beadwork 'love letters' in the same way as the Zulu, certain items, such as the group of three headbands that a girl gives her boyfriend, are specific love tokens; if the affair between a young couple breaks up before marriage the young man must return all the beadwork.

Certain colours have symbolic meanings: yellow for fertility; green for new life; dark turquoise blue for youth; white for purity. Diviners wear mainly white beads; green and yellow are worn by men rather than by females, though fertility dolls are often made with yellow and green beads. Older women's headbands are made only from navy, pink and white beads.

35. Xhosa skirt of heavy cotton with a free-hanging bead mesh overlay and small purses attached. (Museum of Mankind, London.)

36. Beaded hoop ear ornaments (above) worn by young men and girls; and bead collars worn by married people (below). Xhosa, Transkei, South Africa. (Museum of Mankind, London.)

ZULU BEADWORK

In the early years of the nineteenth century, under Shaka, the Zulu absorbed over one hundred small Nguni-speaking clans to form the Zulu nation. Southern African beadwork in British museums tends to be either Xhosa or Zulu. Earlier pieces are badly documented and may be labelled 'Zulu', 'Zulu Kaffirs' or 'Port Natal' (Durban) though this last is not necessarily a firm Zulu attribution.

In the early nineteenth century Zulu clothing was minimal and beadwork might be limited to a few wood or shell beads round the neck or waist. A warrior could wear a string of interlocking bobbin-shaped wooden beads (fig. 3) or leopard claws (fig. 1) as an award for courage. Photographs such as fig. 38 were taken around 1900 by commercial or mission photographers and seem to have been sold like picture postcards today. While the subjects are posed, and their apparel may reflect the photographer's taste rather than that of the contemporary Zulu, they do show the beadwork designs current at the time and how they might be worn.

Zulu beadwork seems always to have aimed at strong polychrome effects. If the colour illustrations in Gardiner (1836) are any indication, Zulu dance costumes were then made in red, white, blue, yellow and green beads in striped and chequered designs. Pieces collected about 1900 include black and pink as additional colours. The range of patterns includes lozenges, triangles and small rectangles in solid blocks of colour, or horizontal or zigzag bands, often spaced out by lines of black beads. The impression is one of vivid contrast rather than subtle shading. Different areas have preferred colour combinations such as green, pink with green, or red, black and white.

It would be tedious to list the varied forms of Zulu beadwork with their vernacular names, especially since a given ornament may be worn in different ways: for example, that consisting of a bead ribbon or string with one or more squarish bead panels could be a neck ornament, a small girl's apron or worn round a married woman's headdress. The range of Zulu beadwork forms is perhaps the largest found in one tribal group.

In form, Zulu beadwork falls into four main divisions. The simplest is the single string worn round the neck, waist, arm or ankle, whether as one strand or doubled several times and twisted. A single string of beads can also support a bead panel worn as a necklet or a small girl's apron; a string with different colours in sequence or with tassels of differently coloured beads is a message from a girl to the young man of her fancy. Bead fringes are an extension of the single-string principle, whether the fringe is of twisted fibre with beads at the end of each strand or made entirely of short bead strings attached to a leather or bead strip to make an apron or loindress. Fringes to cover forehead and eyes are worn by brides as a sign of respect to the husband's family and are often made of beads. Girls wear massed strings and ropes of beads as neck, waist or buttock ornaments, especially since lightweight plastic beads became cheap and plentiful.

Flat beadwork comes as rectangular panels, ranging from tiny ones only 30 millimetres (1¼ inches) across to long rectangular *ulimi* (tongues) about 80 millimetres (3¼ inches) wide by 300 millimetres (11¾ inches) long, worn by men on the chest. 'Bandoliers', comprising either a long strip of solid or lace-like beadwork or a narrow strip with small rectangular panels attached along one edge, are worn by men and unmarried girls over the chest and one shoulder. A married woman may deck her headdress with flat strips and panels of beadwork or with hairpins ornamented with bead panels threaded on wire. Flat bead panels, singly or in groups, are used in making neck and chest ornaments and loindresses and to garnish safety pins.

37. *(opposite)* South African beadwork. (Top row, from left) Girdle, Xhosa; necklet, Zulu; girdle, Sotho. (Second row, from left) Eye veil, Zulu; apron, Zulu. (Third row) Diviner's pipe, Xhosa (above); (then from left) perfume box, Sotho; two snuffboxes, Xhosa; snuffbox, Zulu. (Bottom row) Two girdles, Xhosa. (Museum of Mankind, London).

38. *(above and opposite)* Late nineteenth-century photographs showing young Zulu men wearing beadwork including single and multiple beaded roll ornaments. (Copyright: Pitt Rivers Museum, University of Oxford.)

ZULU YOUNG MEN, S.A. 40,316. G.W.W.

Round beadwork in its varied manifestations is characteristically Zulu. A roll, usually of cotton fabric 10 to 25 millimetres (3/8 to 1 inch) in diameter is bound with thread to make a firm foundation. Beads are strung on to a continuous thread and wound on to the roll at right angles to it. Zulu bead rolls are usually patterned, whether in bands of colour, with white predominating, or in lozenges and triangles, calling for exact threading of bead colours. Such rolls *(umgingqo)* form arm, neck, chest, waist or loin ornaments according to size and fasten at the ends, often with brass buttons. Zulu also use narrow (10 millimetres, 3/8 inch) rolls beaded over half the circumference only. These are joined together; four to seven will make a loindress or belt, and as many as ten are used for an anklet, armlet or loindress panel. Beads are still strung on a continuous thread, but they cover the front of the rolls only, with thread alone showing at the back. Ornaments made of several linked half-beaded rolls are often made with a design of lozenges or triangles against a banded background, and the pattern extends over the whole article (fig. 38).

Many objects may be covered with beadwork, such as snuff containers, staffs, fertility dolls and 'medicine' containers. Most of these are covered with the beads on a continuous string, with the colours threaded so as to achieve the desired pattern.

Children's beads are a single string worn round the waist in infancy and made longer as the child grows. Little boys wear a bead waist string only while small. Girls traditionally wear a loindress comprising an apron in front and perhaps at the back. The apron might be a beadwork panel, a fibre fringe with a few beads, or a bead fringe on a bead cord.

Unmarried girls wear beadwork on head and neck, long necklets or bandoliers over bare breasts, leg and arm ornaments, many made of bead strings, and numerous waist or buttock ornaments, which are worn low down behind, leaving the buttocks half bare.

Married women wear less beadwork than unmarried girls and can be recognised by the pleated leather skirt and tall headdress. The woman's own hair is allowed to grow and is drawn over the prepared form and built up with twine to achieve the desired effect. Nowadays it may be detachable. The headdress is garnished with strips and panels of beadwork, medallions, hairpins with butterfly-shaped or rectangular panels at the ends or the older-style bone pins with beads attached on single fine strings. A newly married woman will wear a bead strip with a short fringe or picot edge to indicate the veil traditionally worn as a sign of respect to the husband's family. Skirts, cloaks and breast coverings are often adorned with bead edgings or bead 'lace' and a variety of beaded belts is worn over the skirt.

Men usually wear European clothes and wear beadwork when they come home courting or when attending weddings or dances. Young men wear more beadwork than at any other time, including 'love letter' necklets, since the more of these that a youth has the better. Beadwork reaches its peak at courtship time. From puberty onwards, girls do beading together so that their skills and patterns are shared and passed on. They make 'love letters' and ornaments for the young men they admire or are betrothed to, and a young man out on a courtship visit will wear a large number of necklets, bandoliers, loin belts, ankle and arm ornaments and safety pins, all beaded.

Changing fashions appear in beadwork as in anything else; one modern Zulu design is similar to polychrome brickwork arranged in lozenge, triangle or hourglass patterns and is used in flat beadwork. Necklets with beads strung in berry-like clusters, spiky 'tickets', lacy strips or long twisted ropes tend to be recent. The beads used were always the round or 'seed' beads averaging 2.5 millimetres (1/10 inch) in diameter, with a small proportion of larger ones for contrast, but now many strings of the larger, lighter plastic beads make neck and buttock ornaments that are cheap, easy to make and colourful. Sweets in coloured wrappers are worn threaded as short-term beads; and the extravagant costume worn by Durban rickshaw men incorporates beadwork.

There are several tribal groups with beadwork styles broadly similar to that of the Zulu, for example Swazi, Ngwane, Bhaca and Shangane. Barbara Tyrrell's *Tribal Peoples of Southern Africa* illustrates some of their costumes and beadwork, hardly any of which is to be found in British museums.

ZULU 'LOVE LETTERS'

Zulu 'love letters' are made by teenage girls for the young men of their fancy. While colours have different symbolic meanings, these vary according to the area, and the relationship of colours within the 'letter' can modify or reinforce the colour's meaning.

The colours mostly used are white, black, red, pink, yellow, green and blue. White is the commonest and equals purity and truth. Black may represent the black skirt worn at marriage, or disappointment and mourning. Red can mean the fires of passionate love, or blood, anger and pain. Pink is a symbol of

39. Zulu 'love letter' made by a girl for the young man with whom she is in love. (Copyright: Art Gallery and Museums, Brighton.)

royalty since Mpande, a former Zulu king, adopted pink beads as his own; they may also mean poverty and a vow. Yellow, in its positive meaning, stands for pumpkins, and therefore a home, and wealth; negatively it means calf dung and is a term of abuse. Green is grass, and thus fields and a homestead, domestic bliss, or that the sender is pining away. Blue comes in different shades, pale, royal and navy blue, and may mean loving fidelity, a request, sky, sea, or talkative gossip. Blue and white striped beads refer to the striped locusts that cling together when mating and 'stay together for life'.

A basic form of love letter is a length of white beads strung with loose tassels (*amatikithi,* 'tickets') of various-coloured beads which are 'read off' in sequence to interpret the message. Fig. 39 illustrates another common form of love letter. The bead panels are made with white, red, yellow and blue beads; the necklet is a rope of white beads with larger red and yellow ones. The meaning is: 'the cattle of your people are as numerous as pumpkins. I watch for you till my eyes go red. I say with my whole heart that I envy the dove that flies to and settles at your door.'

Since such beadwork forms part of the courtship system among the Zulu, the messages usually convey encouragement, sorrow at prolonged absence, despair at the long wait before the marriage date or anxiety about the young man's fidelity. Since the love letter is not an engagement pledge, it is quite common for a young man to wear several, from different girls. The subtle means of conveying a message, and the social context, remind one of the Victorian 'language of flowers'.

Since men do not make beadwork, if a young man wishes to criticise his girlfriend's behaviour, he may persuade his sister or some close relation to make a beaded rebuke on his behalf.

The actual sign of engagement is the *ucu*, a string of white beads 2 to 3 metres (6 feet 7 inches to 9 feet 10 inches) long worn round the neck. After the first day of engagement it is doubled and twisted to make a rope, and tassels may indicate that the marriage negotiations are progressing. Both the girl and her fiancé wear the *ucu* as a sign of betrothal. If the girl is jilted, her friends may throw an *ucu* made entirely of black beads at the young man's feet, and he must wear it at least once in public to avoid being branded as a coward.

FERTILITY DOLLS

Fertility dolls, found in many parts of Africa, are more than just toys. They are a form of sympathetic magic, since childlessness is the greatest possible disaster and sorrow for a woman.

The dolls were used in three ways. A childless woman would consult a herbalist or witch-doctor, who might prescribe that she should carry a doll on her back. An early (1847) account describes how a Sotho woman tended a doll and added to its bead ornaments; looking after the doll was part of the healing magic. She would also hold it when praying to her ancestral spirits for release from barrenness.

Fertility dolls were also a good luck charm for girls. A girl's parents might give her one during puberty and betrothal ceremonies. The girl would carry her doll about and look after it most carefully. If it got damaged, there was a risk that her own baby would die. After the first child was born, the young mother would return the doll to her parents for a younger sister to use.

The third use of fertility dolls is similar to the last, but they are a different type. A girl is given a miniature bead-covered doll on a necklet during her pubertal coming-of-age ceremony as a charm to help her find a husband and ensure her fertility. Such dolls are made of a tiny bottle, a cartridge case or a small roll of cloth covered with beads and often ending in a bead fringe. Sometimes they come as a pair, a man and a woman, expressing the girl's hopes for a husband.

The earlier fertility dolls might be made of a mealie cob or a clay cone wrapped in a piece of leather or cloth with a few strings of beads. Such dolls may date from the 1880s. Another early type is made of a bundle of reeds with a small gourd at one or both ends, sometimes with a single bead string, more often with the reeds mostly covered with beads. This dumb-bell shape occurs among the Sotho and Ovambo. As the supply of trade beads increased around 1900, dolls as well as people wore more beads. Among the Sotho and Zulu the basic shape is usually conical or cylindrical, a cloth-cased core of dried clay, wood, mealie cob, tightly rolled cloth or even a beer bottle which is completely covered with a continuous string of beads in various colours. This string, wound in a close spiral round the body, is carefully threaded to make the desired pattern. Sotho dolls are usually beaded in a pattern of trapeziums and triangles, mostly blue, pink, white and yellow, the colours separated by white lines. Dolls from the Zulu peoples tend to be beaded horizontally, whether in bands, diagonal stripes or triangles. Colours are black, white, red, green and pink, often separated with black lines. The Transvaal Ndebele, whose womenfolk wear numerous bead-covered rings round neck, body, arms and legs, have dolls made of a core covered with similar rings like a series of stacked quoits, each ring a single colour, perhaps white, blue, green and red. Dolls may have faces and heads indicated by beads, twine or fur. Extra clothing, ornaments and earrings convey the loving attention given to these dolls in the hope of getting a real baby.

A pregnant woman among the Xhosa and Zulu will wear a special beaded maternity apron of antelope skin to make sure of a fine healthy baby. When the child is born, charms against fever, teething and other illnesses are added to bead strings round neck and waist. While most babies are carried on the mother's back in a cloth sling (formerly made of skin), some peoples, for example the Ovambo of Namibia and the Lovedu of Transvaal, have specially beaded baby carriers. The Lugbara of Uganda have miniature hoods, often decorated with beads, worn by marriageable girls at dances; these are copies of the larger hoods worn by mothers to shield their babies from the sun and may play a role similar to that of fertility dolls.

ROYAL BEADS

Certain beads were worn only by chiefs or by special permission. Early travellers passing through tribal lands had to pay a passage fee, which often included beads. The chief distributed or retained them as he wished. Dingane, a chief of the Zulu in the early nineteenth century, owned quantities of beads acquired from Portuguese and English traders in return for ivory.

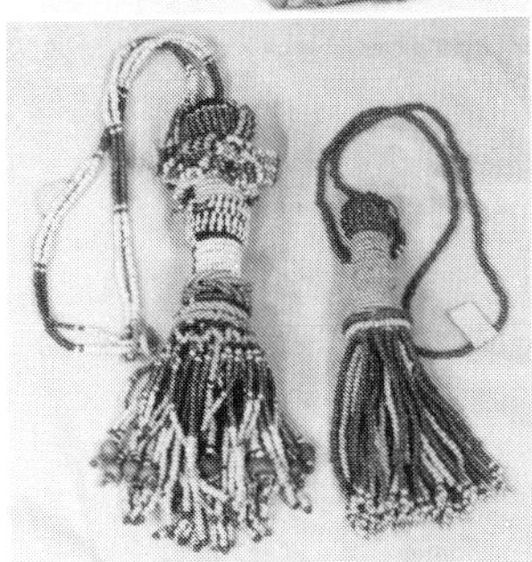

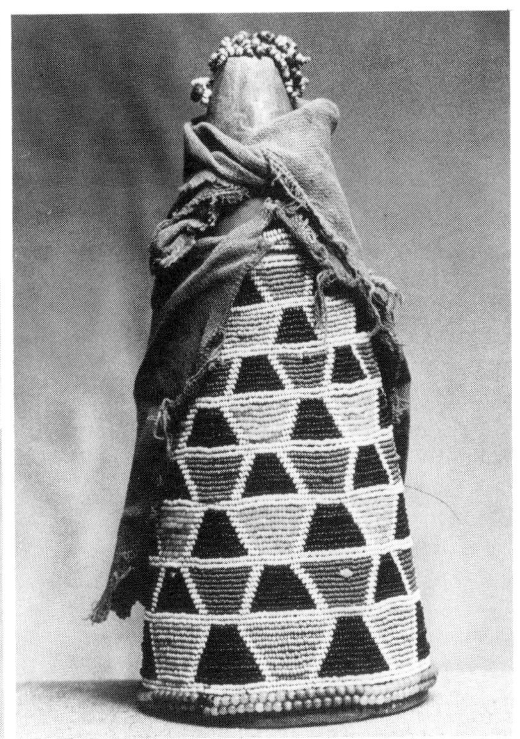

40. Fertility dolls. (Top left) Turkana, Kenya, made from a doum palm fruit. (Lower left) A pair from the Xhosa, South Africa. (Cambridge University Museum of Archaeology and Anthropology.) (Right) Doll from Lesotho. (Copyright: Commonwealth Institute, London.)

Dingane even had the roof posts of his vast audience kraal covered in beadwork; the site, occupied from 1830 to 1839, has yielded large numbers of beads in twenty-seven varieties.

Before the introduction of trade beads, brass was a favourite ornament for Zulu nobility, used to make bracelets, anklets or neckrings or the special beads made for royalty. These are heavy, spherical, about 25 millimetres (1 inch) in diameter and with a straight perforation.

A necklace of large red beads was used in the installation ceremony of a Xhosa chief. Special pink beads, together with bright red touraco feathers, are reserved for the Swazi royal family and entourage. Additionally, bead strings with red, white, blue and black beads in a special order are a prerogative of the Swazi royal family and can serve as a safe conduct. Those wearing such beads improperly may be fined. Royal houses among the Venda, Pedi and Lovedu of the Transvaal also had beads reserved for their own use.

BEADWORK FOR THE EUROPEAN MARKET

Most of the beadwork reviewed in the earlier part of this book was made by Africans to their own requirements. Following contacts with Europeans goods began to be made for a western market. Some were the product of mission stations, where Africans were taught 'useful' skills. In Victorian and Edwardian times, mission schools supplied goods for fund-raising bazaars, and some beadwork would have been included. A beaded plaque depicting the Lion of St Mark, described as 'Kaffir, from the borders of Kaffirland', predates 1884 (fig. 41). It is in the style of Berlin woolwork of the period and must have come from a mission.

In east Africa, beaded necklets, bracelets and other goods are made for tourists. Stools (fig. 42) of the type made by the Luo and Kisii of western Kenya are inlaid with beads, mostly in geometric designs with an occasional elephant or aeroplane. The beads used are the round 'seed' beads, mostly red, blue, green, yellow and white; such stools have been made since at least the 1940s. The technique may well derive from the Kamba, whose stools were inlaid with wire, and later with wire and beads. Maasai women have adapted the traditional warrior's belt for the tourist market by covering leather trouser belts in beads, in a

41. Wooden plaque depicting the Lion of Venice in beads applied like a mosaic, described as South African Bantu work of the 1880s. (Copyright: Pitt Rivers Museum, University of Oxford.)

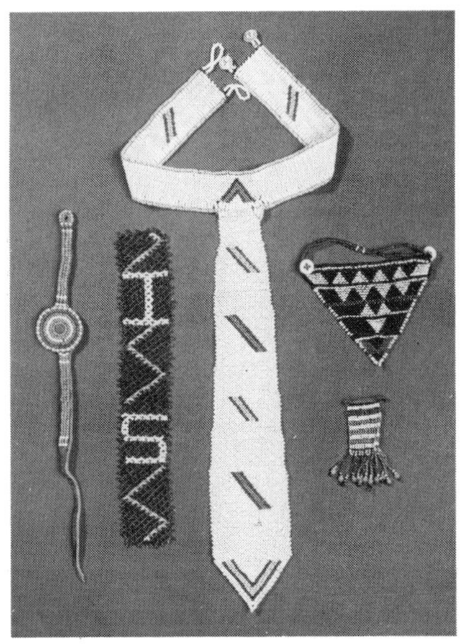

42. Wooden stool, the seat ornamented with impressed beads, made for the tourist market by the Kisii of Kenya. (Museum of Mankind, London.)
43. Modern beadwork. The Maasai 'watch' from Kenya may have been made for tourists; the Xhosa lettered strip, 'tie', triangle and safety-pin pendants have probably been made for their own use. (Museum of Mankind, London.)

pattern of U shapes and vertical bars worked in red, orange, blue, white, green and yellow round beads with some disc beads. Bracelets are made of beads on a leather backing to imitate wristwatches.

In southern Africa, sticks are often beaded. Dancing sticks of the Transvaal Ndebele are sometimes shaped like telegraph poles covered with white beads, with coloured insulator knobs, often like small human heads. Some Zulu sticks are shaped like European crook-handled walking sticks or knobbed canes. The beads are usually wound on in a continuous string to form a design of triangles or concentric bands in the preferred Zulu colours of black, pink, green, red and white. If there are many pale blue, pink and yellow beads, the stick may be Sotho, while a Xhosa stick will be white and pale blue with black, vermilion red and pink. The Xhosa make beadwork ties looking like European ties but a bit shorter, attached to a neckband buttoning at the back. Beadwork bands with lettering could be worn as a sign of belonging to a group.

5
Museums to visit

Any museum with an ethnographical collection is bound to have some beads and beadwork from East and South Africa. The principal ones are listed below. Intending visitors are advised to find out the opening times before making a special journey.

Aberdeen University Anthropological Museum, Marischal College, Aberdeen AB9 1AS. Telephone: Aberdeen (0224) 40241 extension 243M.

Birmingham Museum and Art Gallery, Chamberlain Square, Birmingham B3 3DH. Telephone: 021-235 2834.

Brighton Art Gallery and Museum, Church Street, Brighton, East Sussex. Telephone: Brighton (0273) 603005.

Cambridge University Museum of Archaeology and Anthropology, Downing Street, Cambridge CB2 3DZ. Telephone: Cambridge (0223) 359714.

Glasgow Art Gallery and Museum, Kelvingrove, Glasgow G3 8AG. Telephone: 041-334 1134.

Horniman Museum and Library, London Road, Forest Hill, London SE23 3PQ. Telephone: 01-699 1872, 2339 or 4911.

Hunterian Museum, The University of Glasgow, Glasgow G12 8QQ. Telephone: 041-339 8855 extension 221.

Ipswich Museum, High Street, Ipswich, Suffolk IP1 3QH. Telephone: Ipswich (0473) 213761 or 213762.

Manchester Museum, The University of Manchester, Oxford Road, Manchester M13 9PL. Telephone: 061-273 3333.

Merseyside County Museums, William Brown Street, Liverpool L3 8EN. Telephone: 051-207 0001 or 5451.

Museum of Mankind, 6 Burlington Gardens, London W1X 2EX. Telephone: 01-437 2224 or 2228.

Pitt Rivers Museum, South Parks Road, Oxford OX1 3PP. Telephone: Oxford (0865) 512541.

Powell-Cotton Museum, Quex Park, Birchington, Kent CT7 0BH. Telephone: Thanet (0843) 42168.

Royal Museums of Scotland, Chambers Street, Edinburgh EH1 1JF. Telephone: 031-225 7534.

Saffron Walden Museum, Museum Street, Saffron Walden, Essex CB10 1JL. Telephone: Saffron Walden (0799) 22494.

National Museum of Ireland, Kildare Street, Dublin 2, Republic of Ireland.

Koninklijk Instituut voor den Tropen, Linnaeusstraat 2, 1092 AD Amsterdam, Holland.
Rijksmuseum voor Volkenkunde, Steenstraat 1, 2300 AE, Leiden, Holland.

6
Further reading

Many of these books are out of print, and can only be found in libraries.

Adamson, Joy. *The Peoples of Kenya.* Collins, 1967.
Battiss, W. W., Franz, G. H., Grossert, J. W., and Junod, H. P. *The Art of Africa.* Shuter and Shooter, 1958.
Broster, Joan A. *The Tembu.* Purnell, Cape Town, 1976.
Elliot, Aubrey. *The Magic World of the Xhosa.* Collins, 1970.
Elliot, Aubrey. *Sons of Zulu.* Collins, 1978.
Levinsohn, Rhoda. *Art and Craft of Southern Africa.* Delta Books, 1984.
Tyrrell, Barbara. *Tribal Peoples of Southern Africa.* Books of Africa, Cape Town, 1968.
Tyrrell, Barbara, and Jurgens, Peter. *African Heritage.* Macmillan (South Africa), 1983.
Sleen, W. G. N. van der. *A Handbook of Beads.* Musée du Verre, Liège, 1967.
West, M., and Morris, Jean. *Abantu.* Struik, 1976.

Useful articles and monographs by A. J. Arkell, H. C. Beck, W. M. Cole, V. Z. Gitywa, Carolee Kennedy, N. Knight and S. Priebatsch, Rhoda Levinsohn, Mrs J. Louw, H. S. Schoeman, J. S. Schofield, W. M. K. Sobahle and Regina Twala can be found in *African Arts* (UCLA), *African Studies, Fort Hare Papers, Ornament* (formerly *Bead Journal*), publications of the Royal Anthropological Institute, London, the South African Museum, Cape Town, etc.

Index

Page numbers in italics refer to illustrations.